"All young people, regardless of sexual orientation or identity, deserve a safe and supportive environment in which to achieve their full potential."

- **Harvey Milk**

Silenced Stories

A Collection of PVPHS LGBT+ Students' Memoirs

Edited by: **LGBT United Leadership Board of 2017**

First Printing: 2016
ISBN 978-1-365-55979-2
Palos Verdes Peninsula High School's LGBT United Club
27118 Silver Spur Road
Rolling Hills Estates, CA 90274
www.lgbtunited.weebly.com

For all the LGBT+ kids looking for hope...

Table of Contents

Introduction

When trying to create a year plan for Palos Verdes Peninsula High School's LGBT United Club, their board turned to its' members asking what they would like to get out of the club. Almost every club member asked to hear other students' coming out stories or what a student has faced being LGBT+. Since it would be difficult for students to share their story verbally in a group setting, we came up with the idea to compile a book of stories that students anonymously submitted, that tell their story. The only changes that were made to any of the following text, are grammar corrections or the censoring of names and inappropriate language. This decision was made to keep the integrity of each students' story.

Due to the graphic content of some of these stories, reader digression is advised. WARNING: Stories include bullying, parental abuse, rape, self-harm, sexual assault, substance abuse, and suicidal thoughts.

Ciro Fidaleo's Story

I always knew I was different, but I just couldn't tell what it was that made me different. I didn't play with other boys for the majority of my childhood; I almost always played with girls. I never really liked the typically masculine things. The only exception was sports. I played baseball for five years, basketball for eight years, soccer for fifteen years. I currently run cross country and track. I played a variety of sports, but when it came to toys, I would rather play with a doll than a toy car.

When I played soccer, I played in San Pedro rather than Palos Verdes for two reasons. The first was its close location to my home, and second was that my Dad wanted to expose me to a world outside of the Palos Verdes "bubble". I played soccer with so much passion, and my teammates in San Pedro would applaud me for my great defensive saves on my Saturday games. When I would talk about my plays the following Monday with some of the Palos Verdes soccer players, they wouldn't believe me, claiming I didn't even know what a soccer ball was, due to my girly reputation. That was in elementary school. I just shook off their insults, knowing I could play, even though they didn't believe I could. My life began to split into two worlds. I was known as one of the most aggressive players on the field and a very feminine student on the school campus. During my 8th grade year, I made the decision to switch the PV soccer team. I wanted to prove to the people I went to school with that I could play, and it was also a way to gain some respect from the guys before I was off to high school.

As soon as I switched to PV soccer the environment was entirely different. I had played with kids who could barely afford to play, or got bussed into practice, because soccer was all they had in their lives. These were guys who would give everything they had at every game. As soon I went to practice for the first time in PV, I was made fun of just simply for my reputation in school. It wasn't until the first game when all the jokes disappeared. I played the way I always did, aggressively. Within the first five minutes of the game I got a yellow card for something that was normal in the San Pedro league. My coach constantly complimented me for being the most aggressive player on the field, and told the other guys on the team to step up their game. I was finally able to prove I was more than just the feminine label.

Aside from my life on the field, life in middle school was a daily struggle. Middle school was my time of finding out who I was, but it wasn't in exactly the nicest way. I found out when I looked up what I got called on a daily basis my 6th grade year, I would constantly hear words like "g*y" or "f****t" or "q***r". Although those names did refer to who I was, I didn't know what they meant and denied I was those names. Finally, after looking those words up, I knew those were derogatory terms. In the 7th grade was the first time I came out to anyone, including myself. I was scared of coming out to my two closest friends, but both of them opened up their arms to me with approval stating, "it's okay, we're still friends, no matter what." As great as this response was, I knew I would not get this same response from my parents. A year later I had my first major crush and my first major mistake. Since I was still in the closet, I kept a page in the back of my notebook about a boy I liked, where I wrote down my feelings for him. That is where I went wrong. One day someone was flipping through that notebook and went to that page and my crush saw it. He took it and torn it to pieces and threw it in the trash. Just seeing that just broke me. I was essentially pulled out of the closet that day.

A day later I was called into the office and was charged with sexual harassment. It shattered me considering that that was the first time I had ever met the principal, and it was not on good terms. That day was just a roller coaster. That night I was forced to come out to my parents. My mom didn't care, my dad on the other hand, wasn't too happy. To this day, he is not too thrilled with the idea, but is accepting of me and still loves me. Everything that year just went downhill; my grades, my confidence, and my mental health. I started harming myself, not knowing what else to do.

During my freshman year, I joined a soccer team in which I met new friends. These guys were some of the first guys that have actually made me feel like "one of the guys" and somehow made me feel happy again after such a rough year. But my life, being the roller coaster it is, crashed down, hard. That year the combination of meeting someone and what was happening at home lead to severe depression and suicidal thoughts.

This someone I met, probably doesn't understand the effect he had on my life. I met him through soccer my freshman year and from that first practice, I knew he would be special to me. After about six months of getting close to him, we became what I considered, best friends. I gained feelings for this guy, not because he was attractive, though he was, but it was because of the way he treated me. The summer following freshman year he came out, not only to himself, but to me. Being the aggressive person I am, I wanted us to be more. He told me no on multiple occasions. This started the small tear in my heart that would grow for months to come. We would talk, text, skype for hours and that just became a routine.

In November of sophomore year, I tried to make one last move. From that point he cut me off from his life. This pushed me off the edge from my year of a high with him. About a month later of suffering without him, I couldn't take it anymore. So one December night, I wrote a suicide letter. Six pages of why I wanted to die. I don't know what made me write it but I did. I wrote down everything that lead up to me feeling suicidal. It was not only just this guy that was the main source of the thoughts, he just happened to trigger it. These thoughts were caused by just years of holding back feelings of pain inside. The feelings I felt when my father would yell at me for doing something wrong. The feelings I felt from not feeling accepted by my first crush. The feelings of self-hate based on my appearance. All these feelings got revealed into this letter.

The next day at school I brought that letter to my English teacher. What made me bring it to her that day I'm not sure, but I'm glad I did. I handed it in to her at the end of class, a few hours passed by and I was called into the counseling office. I was sent home for a few days...

When I came back, I was on antidepressants and had a therapist. I was okay with these things simply because I wanted to get better. About a month later I came back into contact with that boy I met. About three months later, I was heartbroken once again because I was told no again. I am not stating this for a person to feel empathy for me but as a way to realize that if a person says no they mean no, not keep trying. This time was it. That night I felt so suicidal to the point where I felt I needed to go to a hospital.

For my own privacy, I will only state I was in the hospital for a week and my parents and sister visited me every day. It was at that point when my dad realized I didn't choose to feel depressed or suicidal. It was then he saw I was a mess and not because I chose to feel that way. He finally understood what it meant to have a mental illness.

Jumping forward to my senior year, I am now a very accomplished student. As a way to fight my depression, I became very involved in the school. I found what my strengths were and played by them. As a method of therapy, I paint ceiling tiles at school to help me release my emotions. Also running cross country and track helps focus my mind.

Although some may find it odd I spent so much time talking about my sports life, I feel as if it is a very crucial part of who I am. It may be 2016 but it is still very hard to be an openly gay athlete. I felt that I needed to emphasize the fact that not every person follows a stereotype. Stereotypes have very defined lines in the LGBT+ community, so it needs to be heard that people do not always fall into a stereotype. I may be gay but I am not as feminine as the known stereotype portrays.

I created LGBT United not only as a way to meet other students like me, but really to show everyone in the LGBT+ community that they are not alone and that the feelings they're having are valid. I felt alone for the longest time but it is only a matter of time before you find the right people to be comfortable around.

I've learned that it's okay to feel different. It's okay to feel emotions, even the bad ones. Although I did go through such a rough time and didn't know what to do, I worked hard to get better. I am thankful for the friends I am surrounded by at this point in my life, without them I wouldn't be as strong as I am now. I may have been to hell and back, but I live everyday knowing I don't want to go back to that point. I did not get better alone, I got the help I needed. Don't ever feel you have to face something alone, there are people like me that are here for you.

What is your LGBTQIA+ story?

1

Being gay wasn't something I always knew, unlike some who have known since they were very young that they are the furthest thing from being "straight". I began to realize earlier this summer, after putting together the puzzle pieces, that would fit together to form a big bi pride flag. From then it kind of dawned on me in a "oh s**t you're gay as f**k" kind of way. Frankly, I didn't deny it, but I was just scared because I didn't think what I was feeling was normal, and because this is a tad new for me, my story is unfinished and presently ongoing.

Since I can remember, the media seemed to show me the "perfect" love story. It involved a beautiful girl, and a heroic gentleman who would seal their love with an amazing kiss and carry her off into the distance on a big, white, horse. Okay, maybe I'm just confusing this with the ending of *The Princess Bride*, but stick with me. After, I would occasionally wonder that what if maybe the girl would want to kiss other girls, and the boy would want to kiss other boys, what then? But my questions were never answered, causing me to be confused when I came to the realization that I am gay. I thought it wasn't normal, because I didn't see anyone else doing it. No one told me that what I was feeling was okay, because no one even seemed to think of anything but heterosexual romance when the topic of love appears.

Eventually, the buildup was something I could no longer hold in, so I spilled the beans to my mom. Even though she isn't perfect, thank the fates for giving me my mother because she gave me such the perfect reception. It was me in tears, red faced, sniffling, in the passenger seat of her car, and next to me was the calm collected woman that I love so much. She told me everything would be okay, stating "You're at a point in your life where you're trying to confirm who you are." She was happy to hear that I was accepting of myself.

So, one parent down, one more to go, right? Unfortunately, no. For the past couple of years my father has been absent, so he didn't get to hear the news. Which made me realize that growing up without a father, even if it's only been a couple of years, is the absolute worst. We all are told of stories where fathers have not been present since birth and single mothers who must take the burden of raising kids alone, but it is a whole different ball game when your dad pulls a Houdini and a disappears on you. Now I know too what this pain feels like because it happened to me personally. And though I know my dad loves me, I wish I could still come home to him like I used to. To be able to run into his hugs, and breathe in the fatherly smell of oil and burnt tires, from his job as a car mechanic. But I'm not a little kid anymore so this right no longer belongs to me.

But maybe there's an underlying positive to that. My father doesn't think being gay is even real. He thinks gay people are "messed up in the head" and that the trans community are people "just wanting to be special." But because I haven't seen him, and because of his opinions, I have chosen to have him not know this part of me. Although it is unlikely, there might be a time in the future when I'll have the courage to tell him.

So I didn't have my father, but let's not forget the one detail I mentioned, my mother isn't perfect. Truthfully, who is perfect? It doesn't seem like anyone fits the definition of perfect. I'm not perfect, Oprah isn't perfect. My mother is not either. We all have our own personal flaws, but sometimes these flaws are bigger than others. Especially when this flaw is a drug addiction. My mother indulges a tad too much in the substance that is alcohol. It pains me to see her do this to herself, and we're trying to seek help for her at the moment. This means that she isn't always there for me when I need her, much like my father.

I hope I'm not coming across as a sad little teenager, alone in this world, with no mother and father to guide her. If you think this, you better pull a 180° quick because that's far from it. Although my home life can sometimes be hard, I have a group of people in my life that make it all worthwhile, my friends. They are the most caring, accepting, and loving bunch you'd ever meet. When I told them that I am gay, they could not have reacted better. They provided me with such strong feelings of comfortableness, that it felt like I hadn't have even told them that part of me.

Now, I'm at a very happy time in my life. Although my story is far from finished. I still have some people to tell, some years to grow up and discover who I am, and to become comfortable in my own shoes. If there's something to take from my story, it's that things will get better, you might just have to wait and see.

2

with one zip
she lets the body bag of skin and muscle
fall to the ground
and steps her skeleton out

there's no point
hiding from the scrutinizing eyes
let your legs and arms clatter together
drumming the melody on your ribs

the streaks you leave on the canvas
coalesce into the blood you left behind
spilt on the white tiled bathroom floor
behind locked doors

they don't see what rhythm plays out
on your crystalline ribs
behind the frosted window panes
a girl of ice and brittle bone

because when the stars hide
you put on your superhero mask
and smile
give one more puppet-laugh
one more show

but at night is when the clacking and singing skeletons
emerge from your neon-fluorescent closets
leaving phosphorescent fingerprints
on your walls

3

I came out for the sake of a bad pun...

4

I've struggled in life due to my parents' background and the environment I grew up in. So I'd love to be there for other people and support them in time of need. Long story short, my mother does not believe the LGBT+ community exists and is just some comedic group to her. While my father is low-key disapproving of it. The schools I went to always looked at me and treated me differently and not in a good way. I went through many struggles and overcame many obstacles, and it is not a fun ride especially since I had little to no help at all. I wasn't aware the LGBT+ community existed until very recently, once I did hear about it I felt relieved to know I wasn't the only one struggling. No one deserves to be alone in the darkness nor go through what I went through so I'd like to help out as much as possible.

5

My story is a little crazy. Not because so much s**t happens to me, although that does happen, it's more about the subject of love itself rather than being LGBT+. Or maybe because I somehow found a way to go back in the f*****g closet!

This story begins four days before sophomore year. I had realized that I was attracted to guys. This didn't make sense because I also liked girls. Little did I know; it was possible to like both but it wasn't until I was eating cereal the next morning, that I came to a life changing realization that I am bisexual.

First, I was wondering if I should tell anyone yet. I then made the decision to tell my closest friend group. They would understand. I was completely wrong of course. At the time, my closest friend there was one of those people who don't believe that bisexuality is real. she kept thinking that I was just gay. Now it was pretty clear at that point that I wasn't just gay. It was a good thing that it was the second to last day before the end of summer. I wouldn't see that group of friends until the next summer vacation cycle started. Those people were my old sailing friends. Due to a lack of PVPHS students on the team, I would not be sailing with almost any of them and will be cutting the nonexistent cords of communication. One of them, however, I would. I was excited that this other person would be my school friend and sailing friend. She also knew that I am bisexual but, she is weird. She did not respond when I told her. I guess she's okay with it. But something about it wasn't right though. I liked her though as a friend. However, she really liked me. We never mentioned my sexuality again. It was now between me and myself. In other words, I was back in the closet.

When school started, I felt like I was in a Jungle and surrounding me were different animals, fitting for PVPHS. At the time, I had no friends except for one. That sailing friend. She was the only hope. One month later she abhorred my presence for a very stupid reason. I was following her around too much. That one time does not equal too much, but I'm not going to get into that.

It was because of this I was able to make friends with my first love. He nor this girl got along with each other, so I decided to side with the boy. I never really paid attention to him until the beginning of November. He was somewhat feminine, we liked similar music, and was cringe as f**k now that I look back. He went to PVHS so it was hard to communicate with him. During a Christmas sailing team party two weeks before winter break, I added him on Snapchat. That night I ended up stealing a gift that he, nor anyone else, really wanted. So I was the one to steal the s****y as f**k gift. That night I also sent him a snap with the picture of the gift with a caption saying, "F**k you ----." He replied with an "I love you" to be funny, but for some reason I really did feel loved. So I saved it and occasionally pretended to type "I love you too."

I ended up finding out that he had a girlfriend and was straight. Don't bother asking me how I can ask a girl out. There was one in my class who I have started to like. She seems extroverted when meeting her, but she is introverted after knowing her for a while. I am the opposite. She was cute, awkward, and funny. Her being awkward also made her very easy to talk to. However, every time I had a chance to ask her out though I "forgot" and when I remembered, I still wouldn't ask. We had spoken before though and at the time, I knew she had a crush on me. It was kind of obvious. Now it was me who had feelings for her. I kept wanting to ask her if she still felt the same way. I couldn't say it though. It would have been awkward if she didn't even have feelings for me. All I knew at the time though was that I definitely liked her. I almost always tried to get help from her in the classes we were in together, so I could be with her.

I ended up finding out she had a girlfriend too. I was friends with her though and she never knew how I felt about her. But I was right in the fact that she had a crush on me because she wrote it in my yearbook. I was actually happy that she had a girlfriend though. It was around this time though I began to realize what how much of an LGBT ignorant environment my sailing practices were. Hearing them talk about bisexuals made my head hurt. I couldn't stand them. The only one who wasn't so ignorant was of course, was my first love. He never used any homophobic slurs, but the others definitely did. One person was even asking why someone was *so gay* as if it was a bad thing. So I asked if that's what he meant and yeah that's what he meant. I don't know how it would have ended if I was back out of the closet to be honest. In that moment, I just thought, "get me the f**k out of here."

The beginning of summer was bittersweet, school and sailing with the team was over, but I had little friends to meet up with so I decided meet up with my old sailing friends. When I saw the biphobe after all this time it was "byoutiful." I really missed her. Looking back, it felt like she was the light at the end of a long, homophobic tunnel. As I got to talk to her more, I really grew to like her. Then I started to love her. I don't think she remembers what I told her last summer, or she isn't closed minded. It took a while for me to realize though that I shouldn't love her at that time. She had a boyfriend this time. The light at the end of the tunnel was temporarily blocked for f*****g construction. What? Me? I didn't care. See I didn't even care. I cared immensely. However, I was polite and did my best not to interfere with these two. But then I saw what drama lied before me. I hated what I saw. Even if that's what it takes to get the one I love. I am not having that s**t. If this is what love is like, then I'm not having it. If that is what having friends is like, I'd rather study for school. That means I give up entirely. I'm too nervous to talk to both boys and girls which is why it is so hard for me to make friends in school. Therefore, I give up on social life in general. So from then on, I secluded myself to my music and the one I love. She was one of the only other humans that I talked to, besides my family, for the rest of the summer. I still love her.

It was because of this decision though, I ended up being more open about my sexuality. I didn't have to worry about my friends accepting me because I didn't have any. Now I am friends with the girl I liked who had a girlfriend and her friends. This story is not so much as coming out story but a series of lightly depressing love stories rooted to my coming out story. Which is still not finished either. I haven't come out to my parents yet. The reason being how unsure I am about how they would react. I plan to wait. I am hopeful I can muster up the courage to tell them. There is also hope in knowing that I have a chance with the one I love.

6

Ever since I was little I felt as if I were a boy stuck in a girl's body. I would want my hair short and hated the way my mom dressed me. It wasn't until I went into middle school that I understood what it meant to be transgender. That description fit me perfectly. I was so happy to finally figure out this dark feeling I had inside of me. Unfortunately, sharing that with others was a different story. I was afraid of myself, I could feel myself collapsing in. when I was a freshman, I finally came out to my cousin after two years of waiting. She was fully supportive and encouraged me to come out to my parents. She helped me through it all until the day I came out as transgender to my parents.

I wrote them a long detailed letter and left it out on the kitchen counter praying that they would take it well. Unfortunately, that did not go as planned. This is where my story takes a never ending dark turn. I came home to a crying mom and a furious dad. He shoved me against a wall and yelled at me saying how "f*****g ungrateful" I was for the life I was given. I was stunned. I couldn't believe what happened. I tried apologizing for what I had done, and I couldn't understand why they hated me. That night, I ran miles and miles to my aunt's house and asked if I could stay the night. She invited me in. I told her everything about how I came out and how bad my anxiety was and how my parents reacted. She took it all in and then proceeded to tell me the only way for it to get better is to get more allies. Which made total sense in my eyes. What I didn't know was that she was later going to spark a night that almost lead to my death.

On a Saturday night, last year, she nudged me and kept persuading me to come out. My mom sensed what was going on and started yelling at my aunt. They went back and forth not only yelling at each other telling each other that they were bad parents, but also blaming me for all the troubles in my life. I ran away from my mom's tight grasp and locked myself into a room where I had the worst panic attack of my life. I felt as though I was having a heart attack. My mom eventually broke open the door, grabbed me by my hair, threw me into the car, and yelled at me telling me I'm never allowed to go back to that house ever again and if I were to come out to anyone else, then I was dead to her. All along this family troubles my relationship problems were not any better. My "boyfriend" at the time though of me as useless and only a female body to toy with and abuse. He verbally and sexually abused me every day. He made me lose a lot of my friends and I felt all the love I once had in my life was gone. I was scared to tell anyone about this.

This is the first time I'm actually doing so.

Back to that night, that was the night I decided that my life was not worth it. Nobody loved me including myself. The next day I ate an entire bag of peanuts.

The allergic reaction happened on school. I was in the pool when it suddenly hit me. I was starting to drown when one of my teammates pulled me out of the water and frantically searched for my coach. I was saved by her. And I'm so glad she gave me a second chance at life. I was rushed to the hospital in a daze of what happened. I was scared and shaking vigorously. That might've been the scariest day of my life. However, there was more to come. I lost all my support; my friends, my family, and everyone I ever cared about. I became numb. Almost someone that wasn't a person. I started hearing voices in my head telling me to kill myself, hurt myself and hurt those who hurt me. I was cutting every day. I still am. Every day I heard the words "dumb b***h", "weird f*g", "ungrateful little pain in the a*s". My mom was using me as her "personal punching bag". Once she pulled me out of bed at five in the morning to yell at me for no reason and made me sit in my bed for hours. I am constantly abused in my household with no escape. My days were filled with yelling, sleepless nights, and countless cuts on my arms and legs. There seems to be no hope. However, I gained a connection with my school peers and my boyfriend. They made me feel like a person again. That's enough to let me continue my life. My scars are healed through other's happiness.

7

I got lucky. Both of my parents are incredibly accepting. I've never heard a negative comment said toward me from a friend or a stranger. I've never suffered from depression or self-harmed. I got lucky, and I am thankful every day for it. This is my story, as a bisexual female.

All throughout my life I have always liked guys. As a kindergartener, there was a boy in my class that I was head-over-heels for. However, like most elementary school love stories, ours did not last. Tragic, I know. Throughout elementary school, and a good portion of middle school, the thought of me liking girls never even crossed my mind. Then eighth grade struck. I would find myself looking at the girls in my class more and more every day. However, I simply brushed it off, claiming that girls looked at other girls all the time. After all, I've always liked guys, so I'm obviously not gay. I thought I just wanted their outfit or their hair or their faces, which is why I didn't give it a second thought. Well, until a few months later when one of my friends came out as bisexual. I remember thinking, "What even is bisexual?" followed shortly by, "Oh my God, what she is describing sounds really familiar". Thus, began the "questioning phase", as I like to call it.

The "questioning phase" refers to the two-year period of time that I questioned myself and my preferences. It really shouldn't have taken me that long, but hey, you live and you learn. During these confusing two years, I would look at girls and think about what it would be like to kiss them, walk them to class, take them to the movies, etc. However, this wasn't enough to convince me that I actually liked girls. I mean, how could I when I've always liked guys? Looking back on it, I think it took me so long because I was scared of my own feelings, and I overthink everything. It wasn't until the beginning of my sophomore year that I finally stopped questioning who I am.

Beware, what you are about to read will sound like it just came out of a sappy romance novel.

I was in English class, the first day of sophomore year, and this girl came in. The minute I laid my eyes on her, my heart started beating out of control in my chest. I still have no idea what it was that caused me to react this way. Maybe it was the way her smile could light up an entire room, or the way her hair reflected the sun and framed her face perfectly. Maybe it was the way she seemed so real, not some girl you see in magazines or on T.V. At that exact moment, I knew I was done questioning, because you can't feel what I felt for the same sex and still be considered completely straight. Next came the hard part; accepting who I am and hoping others do the same. I waited for about a week, just to make sure it wasn't a fluke. It wasn't. The first person I came out to was my best friend. We were in her room and I started taking about a person in my English class --purposely leaving out pronouns-- then blurting out that this person was a girl. Even though I knew my best friend would be 100% okay with it, coming out is a terrifying experience, especially the first time. She just smiled and said that I always liked boobs too much to be completely straight, and then we moved on to talk about her Halloween plans, even though it was only September. This was probably the best response I could have gotten, not only because she was completely accepting, but she claimed that she knew before I did. For someone who questioned for two years, to hear that someone close to me always knew was so overwhelmingly reassuring, it's hard to put into words.

Next came telling my parents. That was probably one of the most terrifying experiences of my life. I was pretty sure they wouldn't mind, but people tend to act differently when it comes to their own kid. My mom just looked me in the eye and told me that she didn't care who I liked, as long as they were nice. My dad just took it all in stride; he was pretty chill about it. Slowly, but surely, I began coming out to my friends, receiving all positive reactions. Sadly, the journey to acceptance isn't as easy as it may seem. Sure, I had great reactions from other people, but then came accepting myself. The constant struggle of being friends with a girl I like and having my mind scream, "God, what are you doing? This is so creepy and wrong. You like her and she doesn't know, yet you are friends. If she ever found out she would think you were sick", but then being friends with a guy I like and having my mind calmly tell me, "Well, this is normal. You want to be friends with a person before you date them, because you want to get to know them. This is completely normal". To be honest, I still think this way sometimes, but I'm trying not to. I'm trying really hard not to. This is my story, and it isn't over yet.

8

When I was a child, I always knew that I was different from the start. I never liked being masculine or tough. Unfortunately, I don't have great parents when it comes to acceptance. Due to these unfortunate conditions, my parents and I aren't very close, but I still appreciate all they've done to keep me safe and healthy.

Apparently, even subconsciously, I love feminine things like teddy bears and pink --I think gender-based stereotypes, such as pink being a girl color, are extremely stupid but we're going to ignore that for the sake of this story. I still have a teddy bear that I sleep with to this day. But, what really intrigued me was a story that my father told me recently. He told me that when I was about four years old, my parents took me to Build-a-Bear Workshop. Instead of maybe building some brown average teddy bear they expected me to build, I built a pink cat stuffed animal with a heart sewed to the front of it. I'm not too sure what happened those years because I don't remember having that bear too long, but I still have it in my house and look back at it like it was the start of a new life.

The start of my story begins in about 2nd grade. I never liked playing with the boys at my school, but I got made fun of if I played with the girls. It was something I had to live with. I always tried to be very masculine and tough and pretend to be someone who I wasn't because I was trying to please my dad. Looking back, I don't know why I did this, but I did. My dad always treasured me like I was his most prized possession. He would always brag about my achievements in golf, how "handsome" I was when it came to family meetings. I didn't really think about it that much. Until I started having dreams. More of visions to be precise.

I can remember these dreams clearly and describe them to you as if I had the dream last night. In simplicity, I dreamt that I went through a silver machine that transformed me from this "boy" that my dad knew into a girl of unimaginable beauty. I had long, blonde hair and amazing facial features. The next day I went to school in my dream, I became known as "Sarah" and sat down in the same seat I had in that class and no one was any the wiser, they treated me that I was no different and I wish this world worked that way. I knew there was something different about me that night. I could feel it. But being the young child I was, I didn't know what to do, so I pushed my feelings aside for my dad and I really wish I hadn't because I could be in the right body that I wasn't born in. I didn't know it at the time, but I now know that in that dream, in that moment, I wasn't the "boy" that my dad thought I was. I'm a girl trapped a boy's body.

I lived the rest of my life up until about 8th grade not knowing what to do. I thought it might be a phase and I would "grow" out of it. The only reason I thought this way was because of the way my parents reacted when my cousin came out as gay and they basically didn't love him anymore. They told me never to be like him and that I had a huge responsibility of being one of the remaining 3 "boys" in the family to carry on the family surname. I spiraled into depression and didn't know what to do.

Last year I started doing research on what it's like to be trapped in a boy's body and came across the term transgender. I learned who I was then and started searching up more and more about it like HRT and SRS. My parents found out I was researching these things and ended up being really mad at me for searching these things because they wanted me to be someone who I wasn't. I knew that when they confronted me. I came out later that year and told them that I was a girl trapped inside a boy's body and they essentially cried and told me I was being possessed by the devil and I shouldn't be acting like this because I was a "boy" from birth and it should stay that way.

At the time of coming out, I loved to listen to Ariana Grande's music and thought it was great. My parents even got me a fan book on her before I came out. After I did, however, my dad forced me to stop listening to her and basically cut me off from listening to any female singer. I'm not sure what's going on in his mind, but I think it's somewhere along the lines of that I'm being brainwashed.

My father even brought me to a doctor to try and diagnose me with some mental disorder and get me medicine or some help. The doctor said I might be going through a "phase," but I knew this was not true. He even explained to me how he experimented with lipstick in college. He also had a transgender roommate, but he never respected her. The doctor kept referring to her as a he and labeled her as an outcast to society. That triggered me in my mind, but I couldn't do anything. After this session, the doctor asked if he could pray for me and I wasn't as rebellious as I am now, so I agreed and he said may God help me get through this "tough part" of my lifetime. Like, what the f**k did he think he could do? Make me feel like a man? Hell no, that's not who I am.

My parents started going through the what I like to call the "denial" stage and tried everything to make me feel masculine, and as always, it never worked on me. I always knew that I was a girl. They even forced me to start going to church. This was the start of a cycle I could not break out of. Every Friday night and Sunday morning. Church. Church. Church. Twice every week. I wish I could just tell them, and in fact I did, but they brushed it off like it was another "phase." This is the start of me being more rebellious. I basically think every time I tell my parents something new, they'll say it's a phase.

My dad got extremely mad at me after coming out and started making me do all these masculine things like working out, going to shooting ranges, and playing first person shooters to make me try and change my mind. I'm not saying I hate all these things, because I love playing first person shooters, but the way my dad enforced them made me really depressed. That made things worse. I also started to alter my voice to make it sound more feminine, but my dad shut that down and always mocked me when it came to even talking. It made me feel like I wasn't part of the family and I still don't, but it made me start to self-harm. I didn't know what I was getting into by self-harming, but I did it anyway. It hurt the first couple times, but then it became a routine. Whenever I got really sad or angry at my parents, I would just pull out my razor and slice a line on my arm. The smile that came on my face was an unusual smile, but it was happy.

I also recently checked my dad's computer and I found something extremely interesting in it. I was looking through passwords of his online accounts, and I found a document labeled as "araoz.docx" or something along those lines and I thought that maybe it was a document for work. As curious as I was, I opened it and the title said "Hypnosis in Human Sexuality Problems." They think that they can hypnotize me into believing that I'm a boy. That also was one of the main factors that spiraled me further into depression.

I joined the LGBT United club this year however and it's made me feel a lot better about myself and that I'm loved, but sometimes it's still not enough. Where I am now, as of writing this story, life hasn't gotten much better, and I haven't been too great so far, but I'm still surviving, so that's a plus. Let's hope I make it through another year. ;*

9

At one point in my life I was extremely down. During freshmen year, I had had enough. I was so tired of being sad and the only way I thought I could fix that was to end my life. So I tried to. As I was laying in the hospital bed with my mom beside me we started talking and getting things off our chest. My mom didn't know why I tried to end my life but I think she felt I didn't except myself. What she said next made me feel so grateful and happy to have such understanding parents. She said " you know your dad and I don't care what your sexuality is, and I don't know if this has anything to do with what happened but we love you no matter what." I knew they were okay with the LGBT community, but the fact that she said that to me made me feel so content and less nervous about myself. It was like a weight I didn't know I was carrying being lifted off of me. After my hospital visit I became way more open about myself to my mom. I told her about a girl that had asked me out and I also said that I was okay with liking both girls and guys. She told me that it doesn't matter as long as I'm happy with myself. And, now that I think about it I wish I had told them sooner.

10

Dear Reader,

I'm especially glad that you've expressed an interest the tragic and some happy accounts of some queer kids. Let this serve as my update from the closet. Enjoy.

I am unfortunately confined to a dark, and incredibly lonely prison. It's the realist thing in existence. Sometimes I think of just coming out and how joyous and gay it could be. But I can't leave, not for lack of wanting to, I just can't come out. I can see others embracing their gayness from here. But my gayness will trigger so much shame in my parents that I prefer to keep it in here with me. Sometimes it hurts to breathe while in here. Sometimes I feel such a profoundly burning self-hatred and pity that I can't even look at myself. Sometimes I think I'll die from the agony of being in here. Yet, sometimes I feel numb and I could just melt. It's awful in here. I have such a great desire to be out. But I know my family won't have a gay child. So, what do I do? I could spend an eternity in pain or certainly lose my "home". Right now, I don't know. I can't see a future in which I do either. If you have any suggestions, you can slide them under the door, don't worry I'll be here for a while.

If you've never been in the closet, this is mine and now you know. If you're out, enjoy it for me please. If you can come out, I recommend that you leave this miserable place and never look back. If your trapped, like me, one day.

Love,
A Closeted Queer

11

Even before I came out, things were not easy for me. My parents had been separated since I was 8, and when I came out I had been continuously dealing with ongoing sexual abuse for four years. I never came out to my parents. I never really told anyone I am gay. I just started dating a girl. In the 8th grade, we were the only openly gay couple on campus. We walked around holding hands and cuddled at lunch. That lasted about two weeks before I realized she had a crush on someone else and was using me to make them jealous. My parents have no knowledge of this to this day. But this relationship inspired someone who felt lost. They hadn't talked to me much before that, and they used a science project as an excuse to get me to their house so they could tell me. They came out to everyone that year, and they also became my best friend.

In freshman year, I faced a whole new struggle; gender. I came out to everyone as nonbinary, including my parents. I changed my name and my pronouns. My parents didn't seem to make an effort or take it seriously, treating it like a phase. I asked for therapy several times with no serious response.

In sophomore year, I found a girl. Possibly the girl of my dreams. She's still with me to this day, and wow have we been through a lot. She helped me and is still helping me make my full transition into boyhood. After a while of dating her, I found that our relationship was more stable than any one that I had ever had before, and I was able to focus on myself and my life. This helped me to come to the realization that I am indeed a transgendered male. She has been so patient and kind. I think everyone deserves someone like her in their lives, especially when coming out.

The reaction from my parents was a different story. They acted like this was out of left field completely, obviously not taking me seriously previously being nonbinary.

I only got a therapist after yelled, "I need help!" at my mom while sticking my bloody wrists out at her, which I only did because I would've died. If she hasn't cared so much about our family image, she would have gotten me to a hospital then and there. She got me a therapist three weeks later, after I consistently pushed her to do so. When I came out as trans, my therapist was in full support of it, especially because I was happier than I'd ever been, having found a huge part of myself and finally being comfortable and not so anxious all the time. When my mom found out that my therapist supported it, she made me stop seeing her. I am now going to a different therapist, who is fine. I just miss my first one very much.

12

I grew up in the Midwest. As a kid, I never really thought much about love or gender. I was me and that was all I needed to know. That being said, I've never really felt like I fit into the mold that everyone sees me in. I've never quite felt comfortable being called "daughter" or "young woman" or "miss" but I never wanted to be a boy. I'm somewhere in between but I'm also nowhere, I'm not even a part of the gender spectrum. I don't normally tell people, since I don't find it relevant, pronouns don't really affect me, so it's more of a personal struggle. I have a conflict within myself, trying to figure out my identity and what to do with it. It's not something you know just because that's who you are. I understand it about as much as everyone else in the world. I don't know much about who I am, but I'm working to improve that and truly represent myself as what I feel inside. Being this way is definitely not something I chose, but it's part of who I am, so I accept it.

Gender is just one component of my confusion. For the longest time throughout middle school and high school, I couldn't figure out why all my friends were obsessed with their crushes and attractive celebrities. I didn't understand the way they would talk about someone being "so hot" and the like. After stumbling upon something called *asexuality* on the internet, I did some research and I am so glad I did. I am now confident and proud to identify myself as 'ace'. I don't experience sexual attraction, but that doesn't mean I'm broken or missing out on a huge part of life. Figuring out I am biromantic came soon afterward. Now I am proud and understanding of who I am and who I'm attracted to, but mostly I'm just glad that I am me, and not anyone else.

13

My coming out story is actually pretty funny. I didn't mean to do it, I did it on accident. My mom was talking about how much she supports the LGBT+ community. She was saying how she supported it the most in the family. And I said "Nah, I'm pretty sure I support it more." Then she says "Well, I have a lot of friends who are a part of the community." We went on back and forth for a few minutes and then I blurted out "Oh yeah? Well, I'm in the LGBT+ community so hah!" She looked surprised and I had realized what I just said. But she started laughing and she said "I already know you're bisexual, but it was funny that you accidentally came out!"

14

I was born into a relatively poor family. We lived in Torrance right next to the refinery, our house was actually a shack but it was home. I shared a room with two of my sisters and next to my room was my three brothers' room. When I was about three, my older siblings moved out. My Mom and Dad shared a room and the whole family shared one bathroom. My mother has always been the harsh disciplinarian, whereas my Father was kind. He never raised a hand to anyone. My Father was always my main support, we did as much as we could together. Sadly, when I was 8, he passed away.

We were allotted a large sum of money by the company he worked for, due to the fact the incident, that was the cause of his death, could have been avoided. However, this was not the beginning of me knowing I was *different*. I had always known, by the way I like to dress, the more 'aggressive' I was, and my personal interests in people and who I found fascinating. However, this time in my life was crucial, we had moved twice in the next year. The first house we moved into was in Rancho Palos Verdes near Rancho Vista Elementary, which is where I continued elementary school. People there were not very kind, I was frequently the target of isolation and teasing. I was never really sure what I did to deserve it, but looking back; is there ever anyone who deserves to be bullied? The next house we moved into was also in RPV by Marymount University, I finished off my elementary career at Mira Catalina. The bullying was worse there, people saw themselves as better than me and thus began tormenting and teasing me viciously. Nobody there associated with me except for, very rarely, a single boy. This caused the children, as children do, to torment the two of us saying we were 'dating'. Little did they know I had no interest in the male gender, I could only see us as friends no matter how hard I tried to think otherwise.

Once that year was over I went to middle school at Miraleste Intermediate, where the torments followed me and became even worse. At this point I had figured out that I am gay and with no shame, because I had nothing to lose, voiced that. I tried to date boys but just couldn't feel the way I did towards girls. The counselor there watched me with close eyes the first years and had my mom take me to therapy. At this point I was smart enough--or dumb enough-- to leave out the part of my Mother's abuse and merely told them everything else; how I had picked up this pesky little habit called self-harm, I had all but completely stopped eating and if I did I would throw it up. And thus, began my first trip to a mental hospital. I was diagnosed with Severe Major Depressive Disorder, Anxiety, and EDNOS (Eating Disorder Not Otherwise Specified) among a few others. They started me on a medication, a week after leaving the hospital they changed me to a different medication, and so on and so forth for about a year. This all occurred while constantly trying to keep myself together at school. The counselor placed me in a group of other kids at the school who had gone through a major loss and we spent almost every Tuesday during 3rd period with the counselor in a therapy group.

However, despite all this, in January of my sixth-grade year my older sister's boyfriend, who had been staying with us, raped me. He raped me another time after that, before I told my mom and had it reported. We later found out he had been stealing from us and had been a serious creep. After this, I began seeing my outside therapist much more often because my anxiety had become very serious. Only a select two people knew a little about what had happened and really, in their own ways, tried to support me. However, I was on a steep and speedy downfall. The bullying became so bad I was recommended by the school to leave. So my mom sent me into a Christian middle school where it was a little better because I hid my true self. I believe it was due to this that I began having some serious physical issues, and I was diagnosed with chronic migraines, a dissociative disorder, and severe stomach issues that would further develop. I fought through this trying not to convey this to other people. During this year, a close friend of mine who also had similar mental health issues, ended up ending her life while over the phone with me by shooting herself. Due to this I still suffer from PTSD, though I have sought out trauma therapy. After that occurred, I attempted suicide once more but failed and was capable of hiding what I had done from my family.

Furthermore, as eighth grade ended I was sent into a private Christian college preparatory that had just opened up. Here people had become more accepting of people being gay and we were all thrown into a fishbowl where we knew no one so I was able to make friends easily. (Note: I was not out to my family yet). In December of my freshman year I met a girl named S**, we met at a small get-together at a mutual friend's house. At this point in time I was to focused on my schooling and work that my mental state was insignificant, and due to that, and my past, I had put up many walls towards people, but when I met her all of those walls came crashing down. We talked for hours, exchanged phone numbers and when we parted continued texting for hours. One issue, S** had a girlfriend at the time, S****. They were not the best couple, they always fought and S** didn't even like her all that much. And she had actually planned on breaking up with S**** the night she met me. Anyway, we hit it off and ended up dating. In March of that year, I was convinced I loved her and she was the one so I asked her to sleep over at my house one night, however one of my best friends at the time told S****, and as a teenager, S**** got her mom involved and had her mom tell my mom S** was gay and she was going to 'corrupt' me. Me and my mom got into a huge argument and as we were driving S** home I burst out that I was gay and that it was not S** who influenced me but merely who I was. My mom forbade me to see her however that did not hold me back.

We met up as frequently as possible and I continued to date her well into 2016, sadly, she had turned to drugs and alcohol and cheated on me while under the influence and then cheated on me sober. I could not forgive her; however, I did want to speak to her. When I went over to her house she started yelling at me saying it was my fault and became, for the first time, very aggressive. I left and since have not gone back.

Moving forward to the beginning of this year, as a senior, I started at Palos Verdes High School because we could no longer afford the Christian school. At PV, there were many people who remembered me from middle school...in a bad way. The bullying began and on the Sunday after that first week of school, I attempted suicide again. This time I tried to say goodbye to all of my close friends and one of them was up at that time of night and called the police. I lied to the police and ended up waking up the next morning in excruciating pain. My mom took me to the emergency room and on the way, I had to explain what I had done. The doctors couldn't do anything so they gave me a little pain medication and sent me to Del Amo. I was there for nine days, and had to call in sick for the week at where I worked. Once I was out I didn't go back to PV and my mom tried to get me into PVPHS as swiftly as possible. Once there I was introduced to a nice girl my age who showed me around campus. We were able to talk and connect and she gave me the numbers of some old friends who I was able to reconnect with. Since I've come to PVPHS I've been able to reconnect and set aside old grudges, I've been able to get a better job and talk better with my mom. I may feel isolated sometimes, however I have hobbies, such as art, that I can fill my alone time with. I have learned how to seek out help and how to achieve happiness even when alone. There will always be bad days but it's important to know, as someone of the LGBTQ+ community, I am not alone in my suffering and if ever called for I will ALWAYS take the time to help.

15

I had my first real crush during the summer between fourth and fifth grade. We were at a tennis camp at the local club. I was 10 at the time.

I met him on the first day. I had no friends there, so I didn't have anyone to hang out with before session started or during lunch. He came up to me and introduced himself as *A*. *A* wasn't the smartest or cutest boy in the camp, but he was the only one who, out of his own good will, tried to make me feel less alone.

After a birthday party and a move, I lost his phone number and thought I would lose him forever.

The most "gasp!" aspect of this story is when people read it and the find out that I am a boy as well. I knew my feelings for him would change my life, whether it was in a big or small way, better or worse, but I knew I would find a way to get through it.

My feelings for *A* brought on a fifth-grade year that was much more difficult than it needed to be. A bully, *B*, decided I was easy prey and spent the year calling me "g*y", "b***h", and "girl", and even occasionally convinced people I considered to be friends, to tease me too.

The phrase "ruining my life" could have been used much worse fashion, and I was aware that hundreds of thousands of other people go through much worse things, but being hurt about something should never prompt people to compare you to others. You are you, I am me, and we have gone through our own highs and lows. The worst thing someone can do for another person who is in pain, is to tell them to shut up because there are starving kids in Africa.

Sixth grade was amazing. Actually, that is an understatement. Sixth grade was a relief. The bullies from my elementary school all went to a different school. Life seemed to be getting better.

I could have mistaken seventh grade as a war zone. I felt fine for the first trimester, but the rest of the year was a problem --a big one. I returned to the question "am I gay?". While it's more than a given now, then it was something I almost rushed to a conclusion for. The first person I told was my best friend, *C*, and her first reaction was to consider me a replacement for her also-gay brother, *D*, who moved away earlier that year. I was touched, but wasn't really feeling it.

I tried an LGBT support group after telling some other close friends, most of my family, and wasn't really feeling that either. I don't know what it was, but they made me feel normal. What I disliked about that was my strive to be different. They almost made me feel like I wasn't expressing myself enough. I went to three meetings. That was it.

Plot twist --I ended up in a brief relationship with *D* and it ended very quickly, which didn't leave me in the best mental condition. The worst part, was that it was the day I was celebrating one year since I came out of the closet. My best way of describing my feelings, at the time of this happening, was a sense of passive suicide.

A few days after February 9th, I scrolled through Instagram, seeing lots of success stories about homosexuals and their partners, marriage, and happiness. I just couldn't seem to let it go. Everything I saved was there to help me get over it. My sister went through them that night. One picture startled her.

The picture was split down the middle, with a red background on the left and blue on the right. A boy with a knife to his skin was drawn on the left, and on the right, was a girl just sitting there. The caption read "which is worse?". I thought it was inspirational, just like every other picture I downloaded. This just triggered something in her. In me. I warned her to hide the knives. She listened. No one spoke to me for the rest of the night. I may have cried myself to sleep.

The next morning, I went back to my mom's house and I didn't feel safe. I couldn't trust myself. I couldn't trust others. My dad called the police on Thursday night. They arrived at my mom's house at 4 AM Friday. I spent the day calling my dad, answering questions, showing my arms to prove I never cut myself. To this day sometimes I wonder what would've happened if *D* had been kinder. If I had never met him in the first place.

A few months of therapy and two tiny heartbreaks later, I learned to keep my distance and be patient. I shouldn't have to worry about who I can trust. I couldn't wait until high school because I knew that people would stop caring about fitting in and just be themselves. No one understood that in middle school. Maybe I didn't either.

Being an openly gay student in high school is definitely not easy, but now I can choose whether I want to care or not. You are only as good as your worst thoughts. It doesn't make me perfect, but of course no one is.

16

For the past 4 years, my life has been quite a wild ride. I went through so many phases, just trying to figure out how I felt about life and where I fit into it. I had a lot of ups and downs during middle school, especially in 7th grade, where I just didn't believe that I belonged anywhere and thought that my life wasn't amounting to much of anything. I was diagnosed with depression, was suicidal, and had severe anxiety. It was a rough couple of years but I soon overcame my depression and was no longer suicidal but I still live with anxiety to this day.

Finding out that I was pansexual, along with being genderfluid, was a big breakthrough for me. It brought me so much closer to accepting and understanding the person I am today. It took quite a while for me to realize the traits I found attractive in a significant other and the way I felt about myself. I always knew in my heart that I never liked to be as feminine as all the other girls and I knew I would never want to be as masculine as any of the guys, I was just stuck somewhere in between. Some days I would want to be more feminine by wearing makeup and tight clothes that showed off my feminine figure, other days I would just want to wear "boy" clothes that were usually too baggy on me and wish for physical traits that were masculine such as a square jaw or muscular arms and legs. My identification with genders fluctuated quite often and that's when I realized that I was genderfluid, I didn't ever feel completely feminine or masculine, it was always a little bit of both but sometimes more of the other.

I realized I was pansexual after a long time of deciding which of my feelings were authentic and which resulted from the large amounts of social pressure that pushed me to act and think a certain way. I knew I was pansexual and not bisexual because I personally don't pay attention to genders when I find myself attracted to someone and I focus more on personalities than the physical properties within a significant other. I haven't officially come out to the entire world yet, I have only revealed the way I identify to a handful of friends and one or two family members but the fact that I am partially "out of the closet" is so relieving. It felt like a heavy weight was lifted off of my chest the first time I told someone I was pansexual and genderfluid. I told my best friend at the time and at first, I second guessed myself and wondered if these feelings were really true but I knew in my heart that they were genuine. After coming out, it finally felt like things were right for once and I felt like I could finally be myself and have an explanation for the feelings and thoughts that I had. So far, the people I've chosen to come out to have all been really accepting and very open minded. The reason I am not completely out of the closet is that either the topic hasn't been pressing enough to present itself or I haven't been comfortable enough to express myself because I know that I might be rejected by people like my parents and even some of my peers. But the people in the LGBT+ community are so accepting and I'm so happy to be in a world with such amazing people who make me feel so supported and safe to be whoever I choose to be.

17

Be true to yourself.
The world is already against you as it is.

"Would Be So Much Easier"

TO BE GAY would be so much easier
this never would have happened if I saw women with lust
not disGust
this never would have happened if I saw men as friend
not a beginning to an End
this never would have happened if I fell in love with her
if I were to be, realistic and romantic
I would never have fallen in love with blonde hair, azure eyes. Him.
but I was sure
this never would have happened if I didn't see a future
and now I have a stitch
actually
I have many
HE was ready to give me plenty
a kiss here, a compliment there, but not enough
HE left
he L E F T
for another and my heart in two
this never would have happened if I saw women with lust
not disgust
this never would have happened if I saw men as friend
not a beginning to an End
this never would have happened
if I were gay

TO BE STRAIGHT would be so much easier
this never would have happened if I saw men with lust
not disGust
this never would have happened if I saw women as friend
not a beginning to an End
this never would have happened if I fell in love with him
if I were to be, proper and prim
I would never have fallen in love with brunette hair, bright green eyes. Her.
but I was sure
this never would have happened if I didn't see a future

and now I have a suture
actually
I have many
THEY were ready to give me plenty
a fist here, a kick there, slurs everywhere
LESBO
DYKE
HOMO
this never would have happened if I saw men with lust
not disgust
this never would have happened if I saw women as friend
not a beginning to an End
this never would have happened
      if I were straight

19

They aren't a boy or a girl. They are more of a boy than Chris. They are a boy trapped in a girl's body. They have a gender of their own. People said this to me throughout elementary and middle school. Looking back, they were right.

I'd always felt like I've been born into the wrong skin. Even in elementary school, I would look at myself in the mirror and it would feel wrong. Maybe I was just a "late bloomer" and magically during puberty I'd grow a penis. It never happened unfortunately.

In middle school, the thought that I'd magically become a boy started fading away. My therapist started making me hang out with girls, since that was considered "normal". I grew distant from my male friends, but still didn't fit in with girls. I did notice girls though. "Maybe," I thought to myself, "I'm gay". But that still wasn't me.

As I entered high school, I started to figure myself out. I wanted to be a male and had come to terms with it. I started wearing suits to school to try to be more masculine and I wanted to cut my hair short. All I had to do now was come out.

Unfortunately, I came out to the wrong people. When I talked to my friends about it, they dismissed it as being "weird" and so I tried to conform to gender norms for the rest of the year.

Repressing these feelings only lead to depression and self-hatred. By the end of my freshman year I couldn't take it. I came out again, but now I had made a close group of queer friends that were more supportive of me.

I started transitioning that year. I chopped my hair off and asked my close friends to use masculine pronouns. That summer was liberating and I finally felt relief from the cis-normative environment that had plagued me at school.

I wish I had done more that summer. I should have changed my name or gotten a binder. I came out to my mom in August. "I don't think calling you 'he' instead of 'she' falls under the category of basic human respect" "Didn't they teach you about sex in biology?" "You'll never be truly male." These comments cut deep and still plague me to this day. That wasn't the end of it either. When I returned to school, I was hit again by depressing and suicidal thoughts every morning. I got to wake up to being misgendered in French every day and all I thought about during those lectures was death.

Somehow, I made it through that year and I decided to make some much needed changes to my life. Finally, after two years of suffering, I changed my name and gender with the school district and got myself a binder. I've been passing and growing more confident in myself every day. I'm finally growing into the man I've always wanted to be.

20

I have always been very different from the other boys. I never wanted to go play sports but rather go play jump rope with the girls. I always felt that I was out of place. I had always had crushes on other guys. I just assumed that everyone did. Throughout my elementary years, I had continuously been called "g*y" or "f****t" because I had a very high-pitched voice and I never hung out with other guys. I remember coming home one day and crying in my shower for hours because I did not want this to be true. To me I had heard for years, from some of my religious family members, that being gay was wrong. I had no idea I was gay, I just didn't want this to be true. I used to think that being gay was a choice and I would tell myself that I did not like guys, and that I was just hormonal. I have never been more wrong in my life.

I remember from 4th through 7th grade I would force myself to *like* girls. I would constantly hang out with them, and I would go over the top to show everyone that I was "straight". Looking back, I feel so bad for everyone I attached myself to. I used these people just so no one would think for a second, that I was gay. When I started middle school, I knew it was a new start and I felt like a new world had opened up for me. About half way through my 6th grade year, I had "liked" this one girl and I remember her boyfriend had told me to leave her alone and to kill myself. I was trying to play the victim card and I said "maybe I will" in a text message, not meaning it but trying to create drama instead. Little did I know that my father had seen the message and he was very upset. I explained to him that I did not mean it and I was just upset, but as a result of my actions, my parents decided that this school was no longer a place for me.

The summer after 6th grade was a big mess. I had started to hang out with this guy who I had known for a while. We hung out a lot and we were such good friends that we decided that we would go to this camp together. Now I don't want to go into detail, as even though this is anonymous it still brings up a lot of anxiety, but at this camp my friend sexually assaulted me. I had told the director of the camp but nobody believed me and as a result, I didn't get any sleep at the camp. When I got home, I told my parents and they were really mad but they didn't know what we could do, as there was no proof and no witnesses. When I had started school the next year, he was there. He and his friends made my life a living hell. During that period of time, I developed depression and I started to self-harm. I would talk to my school counselor about all of the events and I slowly got better.

I began to make a lot of friends and started to move forward from the experience. I talked to my friends, had my fair share of meltdowns, and started to get involved in music. I learned to play 5 musical instruments and I started to sing.

Whenever I had urges to hurt myself, I would do something productive, and I am proud to say that now I have not hurt myself in over three years, and although my depression is still around, I rarely have anxiety attacks and I always have friends to get me back on track.

My 8th grade year was my best in middle school. In September, I came out to my first friend and they were really great about it. I had a great group of friends and I had a guy in my view. I had liked him for his charm and personality. He always knew how to make me smile, and I mean he was pretty cute too. We came out to each other and started talking but one day I made a wrong decision and pulled us apart. I would try all sorts of things to try and say sorry but he didn't want to talk. I was very hurt but I respected his decision and we stopped talking for the majority of the year. Throughout that period of time from then to now, I have developed a lot of confidence and I have learned to speak up for myself and others. My message to anyone reading this is, you are loved, and you are worth every struggle you go through, and lastly you are beautiful inside and out, and you should never let anyone tell you different.

21

Coming out, for me, was a mixed experience. On one hand, I became accepted by my parents. On the other, I'm pretty sure I won't ever be able to come out to anyone else on my dad's side of the family.

I'm going to start at the very beginning. As a kid, I never know what it meant to be gay or anything else really from the LGBT community. The only thing I knew was that g*y was a bad word at school, and the little, innocent child I was never thought to look it up. In my first year of middle school, I began to notice strange feelings towards other girls at my school as well as crushes on boys. I thought that my feelings towards girls was just something weird hat would pass. Boy was I wrong. The following year, I developed a HUGE crush on one of my closest friends. This was also the year that I was in a group that would openly speak of the LGBT+ community. Constantly hearing the "bad" word gay, I grew curious and did some research. That led me to realizing that there was a name to those feelings I had. I realized that I may have been bisexual. After finally learning a term to possibly describe myself, I did some more research, but that led me to some unpleasant discoveries. I saw page after page, picture after picture, of biphobic content. Seeing that content made me afraid of who I was. I thought it was gross and wrong, and ended up repressing my feelings towards my best friend, and any other girl for that matter, for a long time. I forced myself deeper into the closet out of fear of who I was, and it remained that way until the end of my freshman year.

After years of repressing myself, and lying about the people I liked, I came to realize that the fear I had was not right. I had met a few openly LGBT+ people, and began to find myself a little more comfortable with who I was. At this time, I had another massive crush on another female friend, and was hiding it. I remember the first time I came out. It didn't happen in person--which I kind of regret-- it was over text. We were talking about people we liked over, and I very hesitantly sent: "I like ____. I'm bi." After saying so, I received SO much support from my friend, and that helped me come out to a few more close friends over the summer. This time as pan. I had done a lot more research after coming out for the first time, and identified with being pansexual. I was met with so much support from everyone, and I became more confident in myself. Confident enough to confess to the girl I liked, and even better, we got together! (I will refer to her as C) However, this is where a lot of things went downhill. Riding the emotional high of my crush becoming my girlfriend, I was looking for acceptance from my parents, more specifically, my mom. We were in the car and I told her "Mom, I have a girlfriend" expecting a positive response. Instead, I wasn't met with what I expected. She wasn't exactly thrilled with what I said. She wasn't outright homophobic it might have been that she didn't want me dating at all, but she didn't want me dating *C*. She told me to end it, but I didn't. I couldn't do it, I didn't want to lose all of the happiness that took so long to achieve, so I chose to keep it going. Even worse, she basically outed me to my dad. I had been scared to tell him since he grew up in a religious household, so I was very afraid to tell him. She sparked a conversation that I was NOT prepared for whatsoever. Luckily, he was a lot more open minded than I thought and didn't pay too much attention to my sexuality. A week later, my mom asked me again if I had ended our budding relationship, and I couldn't lie persuasively. She knew I didn't break it off and became frustrated. She told me I couldn't keep this going and actually called *C*'s parents. I remember texting her and getting no response. I remember the feat for her. What happened after that is not in my place to say, but in the end, we were broken up, even though we still had feelings for each other. Even though I was absolutely devastated. My one choice to open up to my mom ruined everything I worked towards. This whole situation had a huge hit on my confidence, and it hasn't really come back since. Even now, I feel apprehensive and scared when coming out to new people. I'm paranoid to try again with another girl. After being met with some biphobic comments from peers I was a little afraid to identify as pan. All of this fears mixed with my history with anxiety really has not helped. Things with my mom has gotten better since, but because of what happened in the past, it will take a long time for my confidence and acceptance of myself goes back to where I was when I first came out. The time when I was met with only acceptance and love, and when the hate and disapproval was only something I saw on the Internet.

22

I never understood why it was wrong to want to kiss another girl. I remember when I was in elementary school, all the girls in the playground would make the boys line up and they would choose their 'boyfriends'. And while of course it was fun and games, we took it seriously at the time. I remember gossiping with my best friends about who kissed who on the cheek. And while I had no problem with boys, I never understood why no one was with girls. I recall a time where my friend Madison had dared me to kiss her on the cheek, and through a lot of hesitation I did. We both boasted after about how gross and weird it was, but I never really did know why it was. Later I had asked my mother about it and she had pulled out the Bible and had told me the infamous reasoning; because God didn't intend for it to be that way. And while I was devoted to my faith, my question remained unanswered.

I hadn't really thought about it again until I got older, when things like relationships were a more serious matter. After a very bad couple of years living with my mom under the rule of her new and abusive boyfriend, I went to live with my father in another state and carried the memories and fear I had experienced there with me. I started getting depressive thoughts that 6th graders usually didn't fuss about and I constantly questioned my self-worth. I tried to surround myself with friends in order to deal with these issues, and they happened to be the people that made me aware of homosexuality again. Rather than being Bible-thumpers, they had an unbiased opinion on the subject of boys liking boys and girls liking girls. Of course, being snotty middle-schoolers, we would make fun of it here and there. But since I had been raised to love everyone equally, I realized that it was ignorant to do so. And besides that, the thought of liking another girl was interesting to me. I had always thought women were beautiful and attractive just as men were, but had never gone to thinking that I could like one in a romantic kind of way.

Around 8th grade when gay marriage was being considered to become legal, my friends (most of them being girls) started to open up and realize their sexuality as well. I sound myself safe to talk about it with them rather than with my family, who discouraged it in the name of their faith. It was when I had developed a crush on one of my best friends that I realized that homosexuality might just apply to me, or at least some of it since I still had an interest in boys. I kept my fondness of her secret but was aware of the potential that I could possibly date her. The thought consumed me and I had gone to my stepmom about it, asking her advice. But instead of the encouragement I had hoped for, she shot me down with being gay is just people confusing friendship for love. You're not in love with her, you're simply confused.' It had really confused and hurt me and made me question myself constantly. Why did I have these feelings? Was I bound to go to hell for having them? Did God hate me? Did my family hate me? The reoccurring depressive thoughts mingled with this for a long time and I began to sink deeper and deeper into a depression that I could not figure out how to escape. My father viewed it as a stunt for attention and had ignored my warning signs. We would argue often and he would use my insecurities against me to win the argument, calling me names and ridiculing my feelings. I began cutting and considering a plan for suicide, the combined guilt of the issues with my mother combining with the issues with my father. My only source of enlightenment were my supportive friends and my fondness for drawing which I put my heart into. In my freshman year I began a relationship with my other best friend, which I kept a secret from my parents. She was someone I trusted with everything and vice versa and made me feel confident in how I defined myself. I was finally proud to call myself a biromantic in front of everyone who would accept it. And though I was still battling my depression and anxieties, I did not let them drag me down as much as they had before. However, recently due to my father's job we had to move down to California, was far from where I had lived before. I feared I would lose the happiness tied to my friends and my girlfriend but they assured me that that wouldn't be the case. My girlfriend and I were together for 8 months, 5 of them being long distance, which was even harder for us since I was still not out and I would have to mask our phone conversations and interactions, which would frustrate and sadden the both of us. And though we had intended to persevere through that, it became too much to handle and too uncertain to continue. We broke up two months ago and began to lose contact with each other. I began to become very lonely and isolated again, especially since moving into PV meant starting over with no friends. My depressive thoughts are very high now and I'm trying my best to push through it all on my own. When I found out there was a LGBT club here, I became very hopeful of finding more people to relate to and make me more confident in who I am.

23

Having a significant other of the opposite gender made blending in with the heterosexual community incredibly easy. People are so busy nowadays that they assume and infer everything when given a simple fact, such as when a girl is dating a boy. Straight, obviously. When a girl dates a girl? Gay. When she dates a girl after a boy? Bisexual. Assumptions, assumptions, assumptions. Nobody thought twice about who I truly was, or how I truly felt.

At first, I tried to actively represent my orientation, correcting people when they would assume I was straight and then explaining in detail what exactly "asexual panromantic" meant when I was met with puzzled looks. But without fail, every single time, my efforts were met with laughs, as if one of my defining aspects was a kind of sick joke. They said sexual desires were a part of being human, and that I was either lying or an alien. They said that being attracted to all genders was impossible, and that I was just desperate.

That was four years ago. Today, I'm surrounded by people who can relate to me and support me in all of my endeavors. Safe spaces exist all around me, and I'm grateful for them every day.

I started to believe that maybe, just maybe, I could be who I was and not have to pretend anymore.

I was wrong.

Recently, my own mother, whom I never thought to be judgmental or narrow-minded in any way, looked at me with the coldest eyes I've ever seen before when the words "I'm not straight" left my mouth. Her eyes begged me to laugh, to say that it was a joke. After quietly leaving the room and shutting the door behind me, everything felt cold. The door handle froze the tips of my fingers, the floor gave my feet and toes frostbite. The tears that ran down my face numbed my cheeks and eyes. The warm world that I grew up in, that she raised me in, filled with liquid nitrogen and shattered, leaving me jaded and lost.

My heart of gold broke like glass, and I thought that I didn't want to pick up the pieces anymore. I always was --and still am-- stuck in an endless loop, trying to decide whether or not to openly represent the asexual and panromantics of the world. There's so much hurt and anger in a world where fairness is not always guaranteed, but I keep trying. I cut myself on the edges but I pick up the pieces again and again and I keep trying. I know that there is beauty out there, somewhere. I know assuming that all people are judgmental would put me on the same level as the people who hurt me, and I know that I can do my best to keep trying to make a difference in the world.

24

Panromantic asexual. What a mouthful. This is the reason why I prefer to just call myself "gay" or "queer." Honestly, I would even prefer to just try to pass as heterosexual. I'm scared of people questioning my identity. Of people invalidating me. I imagine feeling flustered, trying to explain to someone what the alien terms "panromantic" or "asexual" mean. What? There's more than two genders? Have you even *had* sex yet? How do you know you're asexual?

For those of you who don't know, panromantic means that I experience romantic attraction for anyone regardless of gender, such as male, female, and non-binary. Asexual means I do not experience sexual attraction for anyone.

My experiences in coming to identify as I do now wasn't as clear cut as others' might be. I did not have a single "aha" moment where I realized that I was "gay since childhood" or "always had crushes on girls," like what happens to most LGBTQ people. Instead, while exploring my orientation, I learned about so many new, different identities and just came to adopt the terms "panromantic" and "asexual" because I thought they described what I feel.

Even though I came out to my immediate family and close friends a little over a year ago, I still struggle with the rest of my peers knowing that I'm not straight. Though my family and friends are accepting and supportive, I am afraid of being bullied or thought of as "weird." I hate being different. Now that I'm thinking more about it, internalized homophobia is the root cause of this. I think a lot of LGBTQ people might face when coming to terms with their identity.

However, slowly, as the LGBTQ community gains more representation and acceptance, I have since become more confident in my identity and not as afraid of showing pride in who I am. Though I may not be totally open about being queer, I am comfortable hinting that I am not straight. For instance, I openly talk with my fellow LGBTQ friends about LGBTQ issues in front of people who may not know that I am queer. For me, this is an important step on the path to having more confidence in my identity.

I am glad to be who I am. More and more people are becoming accepting of the LGBTQ community, giving me hope for a future in which everyone has equal rights. To those of you questioning your identity or too afraid to come out, take your time. Don't let others pressure you into identifying a certain way, you'll figure it out on your own. And remember, love is love.

25

When my parents found out I was gay, it was not my choice. My mother went through my phone and ended up seeing messages exchanged between me and my now ex-girlfriend. It felt as though the baby steps I had been taking to come out of the closet were wasted; instead I was forcefully pushed outside of my comfort zone and exposed to my friends and family. I felt like the black sheep (to be fair, I was), and there was nothing I could do about it. That summer, I traveled to meet my family in England and France, and when I landed back in LAX, an immigration officer noted how beautiful I was and how I must have a boyfriend. I was sick of being assumed straight, so I flat out told him that no, I don't have a boyfriend but a girlfriend instead. He didn't even look up from his paperwork to tell me "that's a shame, what a waste of life." My mother was equally shocked and I was, and with this, she understood what I go through for being part of the LGBTQ community. Ultimately, my family came to accept me, but not before their misunderstandings ruined my relationship. By October, I was involved in LGBT United through the secretary position, and I was starting to feel happier with who I was. By being more involved in the community by meeting others like me and going to events like LA Pride helped me understand who I was, something that had troubled me for quite some time. My junior year flew past me, and now, I couldn't be prouder to say that I am the happiest I have ever been.

Even though this excerpt from my life seems to only cover a happy ending, it wasn't always like this. From the eight to tenth grade I had been depressed and suicidal. It wasn't all due to being LGBT, but a large portion of the time, I couldn't handle not having a clear understanding of who I was. I absolutely hated myself. I switched between calling myself bisexual, asexual, and homosexual constantly. It wasn't until my sophomore year I realized I didn't have to stick with labels. I broke up with my long-term boyfriend because I knew I was lying to myself about being happy and attracted to him. I started dating a beautiful girl who built my confidence and taught me to love myself. So when my parents pushed me out of the closet, even though I was vulnerable and terrified, I felt a huge wave of relief.

Even though they took away my dignity times, and caused me to doubt who I was, I came out of this stronger than ever. I learned that it gets better. With the recent election of Donald Trump and his homophobic VP Mike Pence, I am utterly heartbroken and scared for my community. The uncertainty of how the next four years of living in America terrifies me. Our community has come too far to take a giant leap backward (with a huge shift to the right too). I am prepared to fight for not only my rights, but for those who can't fight for their own.

26

For many years of my life, I thought I was straight. Turns out, I was as straight as a circle. It all happened during high school. Somehow, I had come to the weird realization that one of my good friends was really cute. Except, I already knew he was cute. All of my friends were cute, but somehow, he was super cute, which is why the realization was so weird. I distinctly remember asking another friend about it, asking if I was bi or not, and he had no answer for me. Then came the gay thoughts. My friend - who I maybe had a crush on, probably not - was always the person who would hug you and that stuff. I realized that hey, my friend is super soft and warm and his hugs are really nice. I want him to hug me more. So whenever he did hug me, I just kind of melted into it, and sort of used him as a pillow some other times. Later, during the last months of the year, gayer thoughts washed over me like a wave. I realized that I really wanted to kiss my friend, and I convinced both myself and him that the kisses would just be friend-kisses, because friends kiss all the time (or so my doctor told me). So then I just started kissing him on the cheek, and I felt all warm and happy, and the world was great.

But then the world stopped being so great every time I went to church on Sunday. I remember frantically texting my friend in the church whether or not I would be excommunicated, or what the rules were on kissing someone of the same gender. He answered all my texts and eventually told me to take it up with God. So I did, but I never felt that warm feeling people get, or that bad feeling people get, so I tended to just rely on what other people said. Eventually, I came out to a close church leader and another church friend of mine, and they congratulated me on being strong, and assured me that I could stay true to the church. Unfortunately, because I identified as bisexual (I finally made up my mind on this), they also said how I could swing towards girls more and it would be fine. It didn't really give me comfort, but it's the thought that counts I guess.

Now, back to my cute friend. I told him later that I had a crush on him, and he said that he didn't have feelings for me, which I completely understood. I guess it helped that he still let me kiss him, so I was pretty happy.

Then I had to move, and the world stopped being so happy once again. I used my moving as an opportunity to come out on Facebook, and all my friends supported me, which was nice. However, contrary to my previous expectations, California wasn't so friendly to LGBT people. At least, that was my impression when I got to this school. I heard various slurs in my classroom, and all my friends seemed to be, one some level, homophobic. I remember one of my close new friends look up a picture of two guys kissing, and say how it was "disgusting". I felt very alone, and it didn't really help that the LGBT United club didn't have many members, or the fact that I couldn't figure out when the GSA met. I resolved to never come out at school, and if questions about my joining the LGBT United club came up, I would say that I was just an ally, or that one of my close family members was part of the community. Turns out, a lot of people are school are very cute, no matter how homophobic they are.

On a brighter note, I recently came out to my family and they were all very accepting. I didn't plan to come out to them through a straight joke, but I couldn't resist.

This year is looking better, even with the election that just passed. I have more friends that aren't homophobic, and the LGBT United club has more members than before, which really makes me happy. Although I am scared for the next four years, I know at least while I'm at Pen, there's a community I'm a part of and can fall back on for support, and help support others in turn.

27

It isn't just the media portrayal of the LGBT+ community that can be dangerous. Freshman year was a nightmare. With all of my personality cropping and stresses with my new environment, I started to feel destitute, deplorable. And desperate for something that could let me feel less disgusting, I began the process of going online and showing my body to anyone who wanted to see. This became a habit, a daily event, like clockwork. My parents would go to bed, I would open my computer. My messages flooded with random numbers that I would need to flush out nightly. These people would let me abuse myself emotionally over camera, then drop me into my already deep depressive pit. The entire time, I started to feel like my sole purpose was whoreing myself out over the internet, and my self-esteem plummeted. This went on for several months, thrusting me into depression and mania and robbing me of what I felt was my humanity. Some of these people which I exposed myself for were above 18, and I felt so desolate that I forced myself not to care. People so readily manipulated me, lost and terrified for their own sick needs. That year was my lowest point emotionally. And in one specific moment, someone witnessed that and used it to commit the most heinous of crimes.

28

So not all of my coming out moments were that great. Some of them were not so great. When I told my friend that I was bisexual, she just stared at me and said "you're kidding, right?" and I said no. and she goes "are you serious? I don't think we can be friends anymore! that's disgusting." so... that hurt.

29

When I first came out my mom asked me "are you lesbian or bisexual?" Having identified as pan, it felt weird not being able to come out as who I really was. It turned out it was just a problem of she wasn't educated on other orientations, so it was an easy fix.

Now I'm slightly questioning my gender identity. I'm beginning to like the thought and feel more comfortable with non-binary orientations but I'm not entirely sure. Plus some my friends are not exactly the most supportive of non-binary orientations.

30

Straight up, it's hard to be gay. And not just in the closet life or the postmortem of that period; as an LGBT+ individual under eighteen life simply takes a completely new perspective from that of the main batter for the New York Hets. Having come out to a supportive network of friends, my struggles with the world surrounding my sexuality didn't really lie in that friendship realm. Of course, the process of sorting out one's own gender and sexuality is inherently arduous and is something that I still deal with to this day. That said, the difficulties of living life gaily manifest more in the ways which the outside world has proven especially dangerous for young gay individuals.

When I was in eighth grade, I came out to a newfound friend while at a Thanksgiving party. As he was friends with my cousin and went to school with her, the news naturally made its way straight back to her, and in turn, my aunt and uncle. By Christmas, my uncle was asking for me to go on a walk and talk to him about "something he had found out". Once I had learned the subject my uncle planned on addressing, fear instantly seized my mind; thoughts like 'oh God I hope he doesn't tell my parents' (I wasn't out to them at the time) and 'OH GOD I hope he doesn't tell my goddamn parents' frothed in my head-on repeat and spilled out into the redness of my cheeks and the shakiness of my legs. I was bordering a full-blown anxiety attack. Those thoughts continued to fly through my mind during the conversation my uncle and I had walking around the block, and they distracted me quite a bit from the message he had been trying to get across. He talked about the safety of the LGBT+ community and how there were a lot of people who could possibly abuse me or hurt me simply because I was gay. He was just trying to look out for my wellbeing. In hindsight, my life would be a great deal better if I had listened to him.

Starting high school, I wandered the halls of Peninsula full of zeal and hope, thinking I was prepared for whatever the world could throw at me. Clearly I was wrong, because before long the creeping thoughts of 'everyone is judging you because you're gay', 'why are you so disgusting on the inside and out', 'you will never be what a gay man should be', etc. pervaded my head. I began to obsess over these ideas, especially the latter of my examples. Society tends to create a very stereotyped image of what a gay man is supposed to look like, sit like, eat like, talk like, and act like, and ignores everyone outside of this norm. While in retrospect I know that these social etiquettes that seem only to apply to gay men are ridiculous, fueled by the media's desire to appeal to a demographic by capitalizing on the most easy to publicize and exploit image of the LGBT+ community, the flaming white thin gay twink, ninth-grade me was a ways away from coming to this conclusion. I forced myself around these standards, trying to will myself thinner, trying to make my image Extremely Gay™ and not much else. I shoved my personality into a very confining (but neat) box, and when bombarded with comments like "You're so g*y, I love that," I had no choice but to take them as compliments, as that part of myself was the only portion I really displayed. I've grown comfortable living up to portions of that stereotype since then, but realizing that I don't need to embody the unfaceted portrait of a Gay Man took a lot of time and a lot of work. And being comfortable in the LGBT+ community has allowed me to make some amazing connections with people and help people who are struggling with the same issues I did.

31

From a young age, I always looked at girls differently; I looked at girls the way girls my age looked at guys. I mean don't get me wrong I still saw guys in the same light but I mostly liked them because I felt that's what I was supposed to do. Of course, at the time I didn't realize that. Looking back at it is when I noticed I've always thought of girls in a more than friendly way.

I've never been particularly comfortable with myself, not with my looks and certainly not with my personality. Since elementary school, I guess I never was like the other girls, although I wanted to be. I've always wanted to be one of those pretty girls who was good at makeup and dressed nicely. Throughout elementary and all the way to middle school, and now too I guess, I've dressed in a way that could be considered dykeish, not all the time but a majority. I use to get defensive when people would tell me I looked like a d**e because as far as I knew I was straight.

By middle school I didn't have many friends; I had left my friends from elementary, due to unrelated reasons, and I mean sure I had other friends but not close friends. I made new friends and all but I just remember feeling alone all the time. At the time, I wasn't aware of what having depression was but I can recall I had all the symptoms. Seventh grade was when it all went downhill. I hated absolutely everything about myself. I couldn't stand to look at myself or even be around myself. I felt guilty for pretty much everything all the time, still do, but I know how to cope with it now. I had this horrible image of myself and my thoughts bullied me 24/7. I was a horrible person who didn't deserve to exist, and the fact that I had a good life made me feel even worse. I didn't deserve anything I had or any kindness given to me. I needed to punish myself somehow so that's when I turned to self-harm. I couldn't stand feeling constantly uncomfortable with myself, with my looks, with my personality, and with the way I thought of girls knowing I'm not supposed to have thoughts like that. During that time, I was going through a bit of an emo phase and wore bracelets up to my elbows which helped hide them. At the time, I constantly had things to do and cutting was just another thing added to the list: Wake up, cut, go to school, get home do homework, go to soccer, cut, shower, cut again, clean up, go to bed and repeat.

I felt so alone all the time. I use to leave class to cry in the bathroom stalls just to go back to class and be made fun of for being in the bathroom for so long. I would get made fun of at school for dressing/being emo and all the girls on my soccer team of the time hated me for reasons I didn't know. I relied heavily on my best friend at the time and even though she didn't understand what I was going through, she was one of the only things keeping me together. Without her I would've collapsed but even at that, I just got worse. Soon my arms weren't enough and I needed more punishment and then my thighs were covered; playing soccer, which was one of the only things keeping me from doing more irrational things, was hard because it was hard to hide cuts when you have to wear shorts. And eventually I couldn't deal with it anymore and I had to tell my mom. Twice a week I started going to therapy, that's when I was diagnosed with Depression. Things were starting to look up.

I've always been very touchy-feely with all my girlfriends and we would always joke about how I'm gay. I never had a problem with that, seeing as I had a boyfriend at the time, but later I realized I enjoyed being affectionate with one friend in particular more than I did with my boyfriend. Looking back, I realized I had a bit of a crush on that particular friend but at the time I didn't know; I was just confused about my feelings for her. Of course, I knew I liked her as a friend but my feelings felt stronger than that but I could never pinpoint what it was. I had a boyfriend; I had to be straight right? The summer going into high school I did a lot of thinking and I finally came to terms with myself, I am bisexual. Coming out to myself made me feel a bit more comfortable with myself. I mean don't get me wrong I still hated myself but knowing that my thoughts and feeling about girls were valid and not wrong helped me a lot.

Eventually, I started to come out to my friends one by one and all of them were accepting which made me feel overjoyed. I was especially nervous coming out to my soccer friends, we change in a locker room together-- would they treat me differently? They were all just as accepting and I can't describe how happy I was that they didn't treat me differently, they didn't avoid me in the locker room and treated me the same which feels great. I'm not going to lie and say everything is great now. Being openly out is never easy for anyone. As an out bi girl, I have to constantly worry about if my friendly gestures are taken the wrong way and are perceived as me hitting on them; which sucks because if a straight girl did the same gesture, they would think nothing of it but the fact that I'm bi changes things but oh well. People I don't even know personally don't like me for my sexual orientation, and it makes me sad but I can't change that. Although I'm still in therapy I can say I've been clean for about a year now and coming out is one of the best decisions I've made. Even though things aren't perfect, I'm more at peace with myself than I was, I never saw myself getting out of that horrible place in my head. I've come to terms who I am as a person and realized I can't change who I am so I might as well try and make the best of it.

32

Reflecting on it now, I've always known that I was different in some way regardless of me not really having realized it until now. Growing up, I had always been attracted to boys. I distinctly remember having the butterflies when I would have conversations with those I called "crushes". I was developing feelings for boys in my grade based on what I had seen in my life in terms of relationships, that was just what was normal. When I began getting butterflies for developing crushes on some of the girls in my grade, I think it was easy to overlook it because I didn't understand it and simply didn't think anything of it. However, my sexuality hasn't ever been anything that I've struggled with the way many members of the LGBT+ community unfortunately have; as my sense of self-hood has only grown through getting older and having learned to love myself. Both of these factors have led me to come to the conclusion that I simply am who I am; someone who had so much love in them that they could fall in love with a person regardless of gender. Though many people like to discredit my sexuality either because most my relationships have been heterosexual or the lack of believing it as even a possibility. I am d**n PROUD to be who I am and know that there isn't any right or wrong way to be bisexual, I love who I am as well as the legacy of love that is being part of this community.

What is something you want other
LGBTQIA+ students to know?

"Things may be rough, but we're all somewhere over the rainbow, so try to reflect upon yourself and emanate who you truly are, not a colorless reflection of who you're trying to be"

"Just be you and don't let anyone ruin your vibes"

"Coming out is a big deal, but it doesn't have to be a serious affair."

"I'm always there for others and I would love to help out as much as possible. I'm always available for anyone to talk to whether it be a small rant about how much they hate carrots or something that deals with court."

"I want other LGBT+ students to know that it's okay not to be completely sure of who you are or who you like, and that sexuality is fluid. At one point in your life you may believe you are a certain sexuality, and at another point you may think you are something else, and that's okay. Don't let anyone tell you that you are just "going through a phase" or you are "too young to know". Even if you are just going through a phase, so what? It is your life; you know how you feel and you don't have to prove it to anyone. Feelings can change. You can change as a person, and that is okay. You can't be wrong in how you feel."

"The LGBT+ community can be a truly very terrifying place; I have learned that firsthand. It provides a great resource network, and can provide a lot of fun at times, but it is not territory to stride through headstrong and blind. It leaves its mark on every one of its individuals, not necessarily a bad one but not usually a good one. It left me contorted and abused. It threw me into the street and left me for birds of prey to tear me apart. But I survive, and I persist, and I will continue to help it thrive as best as I can."

"Sometimes coming out is messy, sometimes it feels like you get more s**t for it than its worth, and I understand that. But trust me when I say that any s**t you get for coming out is s**t you don't deserve. Being comfortable should not come at a price. Coming out is worth every second of it even if that means some rejection. You will find safe places and safe people, and make small homes for yourself that you feel comfortable in. Things will slowly get easier. I promise."

"If you are going down a long tunnel don't just expect the light to be there. One must be prepared to have no light and still move on."

———————～———————

"Stay true to yourself. Don't let anyone else influence you. Try to find the good in every day."

———————～———————

"I'd like other LGBT+ students to know that you're always loved and there are people out there who accept you. Don't listen to what the other people say. Be yourself!"

———————～———————

"It sucks, but it's really nice."

"Openly coming out as being part of LGBT+ community might not be as easy as my story portrayed it to be because everyone's situation is different. Don't be afraid to express yourself and don't be afraid to accept and acknowledge any feelings or thoughts that are out of the ordinary. There's nothing wrong with being a part of the LGBT community, it's a part of who you are and who you will always be. Don't ever feel pressured to "label" yourself with any titles that express your sexuality or gender, you don't need to sort out all your feelings just yet, because you've got your whole life to figure it out! I am so honored to be a part of such an incredible community that is made of such marvelous people. I am so glad to have this loving and supporting family for the rest of my life and I am thankful for each and every one of you and I wish you all luck and happiness along with wellness on your wonderful journey through life!"

"It's okay to be you!! You don't have to be out to anyone, just understand and accept who you are and the rest will come in due time. Know that not everything needs a label and it's okay to be confused about who you are. You have time and there are people out there to support you through your journey. Take your time and be yourself."

"I want other LGBT+ students to know that you should never let anyone force you to come out. You do it when you're ready. When you feel ready. Never ever let anyone else decide for you whether you are ready or not."

"I want other LGBT+ students to know that it's ok. Yes, parents aren't always the best, but sometimes it just takes some time for them to really accept you. And if they don't, there are friends and other people that will. I know that I will always be there to support those that need it."

"I would never want somebody to feel the way I felt during freshmen year. And I think the best thing to do is talk to someone. Don't be afraid to open up and get help. You guys are worth it."

"You don't have to conform to society's standards of being normal. Be different and be you."

"You are not alone, you are never alone, all you have to do is reach out and be wholly honest with those who are there to help."

"Quite honestly, people hear it all the time, but it really does get better. You are not alone in your fight. Please stay strong."

"To others who are struggling with their own stability with themselves like me, remember that no one else can define who you are. Only you can. Surround yourself in people who love you and accept you for who you truly are. Never doubt yourself. You are amazing just the way you are."

"I want other LGBT+ students to know that no matter what they believe, there will always be someone who cares/supports them, whether that's a family member, friend, or even a teacher. Also, like I said in my essay, take your time to discover yourself and don't let others pressure you into thinking you're one thing or another. Be proud of your identity, no matter what it is."

"To all other LGBT+ students struggling with their religion and their identity, God does love and care about you, and anyone who tells you otherwise can f**k off, because they're clearly not living the way Christ would."

"Be safe, don't worry, everything will be fine."

"You are never alone, and you never deserve hate or isolation. There will always be people around to help, all you need to do is ask."

"You are not alone. You are never alone."

"You're going to want to give up, but trust me. You'll be so glad you didn't."

Acknowledgements

First, we would like to thank every single student who contributed a story or quote to this book. We understand how difficult it was to write these stories even when completely anonymous but just know that you may have unknowingly helped another student.

We would also like to thank our club advisor, Mr. Mullen, who has put in so much time, effort, and faith to help our club succeed. He has been there since the club was just an idea, lending a hand whenever possible. On countless occasions, he has helped make PVPHS feel like a comfortable environment for many LGBT+ students. Mr. Mullen has shared stories of his Catholic background, which helped many LGBT+ students feel safer around religious groups and not feel threated by them. He would also provide his outside knowledge at the club meetings, such as his insight on the LGBT+ community from a slightly older generation's point of view. Without Mr. Mullen's professional advice on how to help make this club as productive as it is now, we might not be nearly as successful.

We also want to thank Mr. Farrell, Miss Lopez, and every other staff member in the counseling office who helped our club's dreams become realities. We know how much you all care about the students at PVPHS and LGBT United wants to make sure that your constant help doesn't go unrecognized.

Our final thanks go to Mr. Cohen, who fought hard to make sure that the full story of *The Laramie Project* was told at PVPHS, only cutting out a single word from the script. As LGBT+ community members, we know our history is mostly hidden from the public eye but by just putting on this production, you have now helped educate both old and new generations of some of the realities an LGBT+ student might face. You and the play's cast and crew have brought the Laramie event back into relevance, which will speak for itself in years to come.

I, Ciro Fidaleo, would like to thank my current board of LGBT United. I'd like to thank my copresident, Annabelle David, who stepped up and helped me make this a very successful club. Thank you, Tori, Will, Natalia, and Catherine who took on the challenge of putting in so much hard work and effort in order to do what was best to help improve the youth LGBT+ environment in our small community. You not only mean the world to me but also the world of so many students at our school. For that, I cannot thank you each enough.

Project Semicolon

authors use a semicolon to end a sentence but chose to

keep  going

peopele who are still here after being suicidal are on the otherside of what they thought was their end but

kept going...

and so can you.

#ProjectSemicolon

www.ingramcontent.com/pod-product-compliance
Lightning Source LLC
Chambersburg PA
CBHW020340290526
45785CB00005B/2109